HAPPINESS

Laughing Elephant   MMXVI

Happiness

by Harold Darling

Laughing Elephant · Seattle   MMXVI

LAUGHING ELEPHANT
3645 INTERLAKE AVENUE NORTH
SEATTLE, WASHINGTON, 98103

ISBN/EAN: 9781514900352

COPYRIGHT © 2016, BLUE LANTERN STUDIO
FIRST PRINTING • PRINTED IN CHINA. ALL RIGHTS RESERVED

LAUGHINGELEPHANT.com

This Book Is Dedicated To

Harold Darling
1932 – 2016

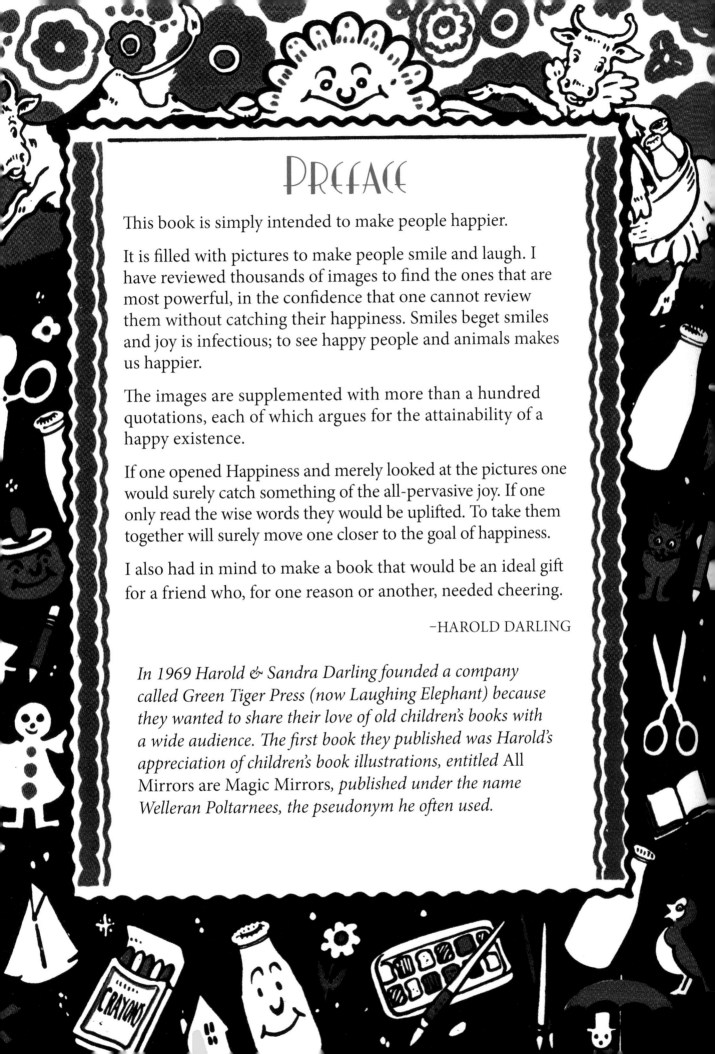

Preface

This book is simply intended to make people happier.

It is filled with pictures to make people smile and laugh. I have reviewed thousands of images to find the ones that are most powerful, in the confidence that one cannot review them without catching their happiness. Smiles beget smiles and joy is infectious; to see happy people and animals makes us happier.

The images are supplemented with more than a hundred quotations, each of which argues for the attainability of a happy existence.

If one opened Happiness and merely looked at the pictures one would surely catch something of the all-pervasive joy. If one only read the wise words they would be uplifted. To take them together will surely move one closer to the goal of happiness.

I also had in mind to make a book that would be an ideal gift for a friend who, for one reason or another, needed cheering.

–HAROLD DARLING

In 1969 Harold & Sandra Darling founded a company called Green Tiger Press (now Laughing Elephant) because they wanted to share their love of old children's books with a wide audience. The first book they published was Harold's appreciation of children's book illustrations, entitled All Mirrors are Magic Mirrors, *published under the name Welleran Poltarnees, the pseudonym he often used.*

Happiness

Happiness not in another place, but in this place…
Not for another hour, but this hour.

Walt Whitman

There is one kind of laugh that I always did recommend; it looks out of the eye first with a merry twinkle, then it creeps down on its hands and knees and plays around the mouth like a pretty moth around the blaze of a candle, then it steals over into the dimples of the cheeks and rides around in those little whirlpools for a while, then it lights up the whole face like the mellow bloom on a damask rose, then it swims up on the air, with a peal as clear and as happy as a dinner-bell, then it goes back again on gold tiptoes like an angel out for an airing, and it lies down on its little bed of violets in the heart where it came from.

Josh Billings

Happiness

Write it on your heart that every day is the best day of the year.

Ralph Waldo Emerson

If you ever find happiness by hunting for it, you will find it as the old woman did her lost spectacles, safe on her own nose all the time.

Josh Billings

HAPPINESS

I felt the way popcorn kernels must feel when they're sizzling.

Sylvia Peck

An animal is nothing more than a parcel of joy. Everything loves being, and all beings rejoice in it. It is joy that when it is succulent you call fruit, and when it sings you call bird.

Assuredly, all nature informs us that man is born for happiness. It is the striving for sensual pleasure which germinates the plant, fills the hive with honey and the human heart with kindness.

André Gide

Happiness

The art of being happy is the art of discovering
the depths that lie in the daily common things.

J. Brierly

Happiness is the only good.
The place to be happy is here.
The time to be happy is now.
The way to be happy is to make others so.

Robert Ingersoll

F. E. Schoonover

HAPPINESS

They who bring sunshine to the hearts of others cannot keep it from themselves.

James M. Barrie

Happiness not in another place, but in this place…
Not for another hour, but this hour.

Walt Whitman

Happiness

Nobody can be uncheered with a balloon.

A.A. Milne

I want to jump and shout aloud in gratitude at having been allowed to live in this world, sharing with its creatures the blessed gift of life.

Malcolm Muggeridge

Happiness

We are all of us fellow passengers on the same planet and we are all of us equally responsible for the happiness and the well-being of the world in which we happen to live.

Hendrik Willem van Loon

They smile at the earth which sustains them; they smile at the air which bathes them; they smile at the light which each one sees in the eyes of the other.

Anatole France

HAPPINESS

Coincidences (even those created artificially), a chance encounter with a friend I have not seen for a long time, the taste of apricots, the discovery of a book I have been searching for, the light at dusk at this time of year, the sound of the wind in the chimney, utter quiet and darkness before falling asleep: all these are for me unexpected moments of happiness. But there are other happy moments attached to nothing: to no event, no particular thought, no pleasing sensation. A feeling utterly ignorant of its causes, silent and sudden and overwhelming.

Alberto Manguel

Happiness is as a butterfly which, when pursued, is always beyond our grasp, but which if you will sit down quietly, may alight upon you.

Nathaniel Hawthorne

How good is man's life, the mere living!
how fit to employ
All the heart and the soul and the senses
forever in joy!

Robert Browning

If your whole world is upside down and joy and cheer are far from you, romp for an hour with a six-year old child and see if its laughter and faith are not veritable sign posts on The Road to Happiness.

Gladys Harvey-Knight

HAPPINESS

HAPPINESS

Let us open up our natures, throw wide the doors of our hearts
and let in the sunshine of good will and kindness.

Orison S. Marden

It is natural to imagine that the best way to be happy is to secure good things for
ourselves. In truth the surest path is kindness.

Welleran Poltarnees

Happiness

Man is made for happiness
as a bird is made for flight.

Polish proverb

W. HEATH ROBINSON

Everywhere there was the stirring of nature and a flashing of lights and an air of celebration. I felt so cool and so happy that I could have taken wing and sailed from the mountainside right out into the glorious landscape below.

Joseph von Eichendorff

Happiness

Sometimes happiness is a simple thing. For no particular reason it rises within us, and we smile or turn cartwheels in our gladness.

Welleran Poltarnees

There is no limit to the amount of happiness we can hold, but sometimes, when we are enormously happy, it swells within us, and we feel as if we were filled with bubbles or balloons, and we must run or leap to let them out.

Welleran Poltarnees

HAPPINESS

Simplicity, clarity, singleness: these are the attributes that give our lives power and vividness and joy.

Richard Halloway

Men are made for happiness, and anyone who is completely happy has a right to say to himself: "I am doing God's will on earth."

Anton Chekhov

HAPPINESS

Happiness consists in activity. Such is the constitution of our nature. It is a running stream, and not a stagnant pool.

J.M. Good

The principle duty which a parent owes to a child is to make him happy.

Anthony Trollope

HAPPINESS

When one is happy one does not hear the clock strike.

German Proverb

Happiness, at least, is not solitary; it joys to communicate; it loves others, for it depends on them for its existence; it sanctions and encourages all delights that are not unkind in themselves.

Robert Louis Stevenson

Happiness

When on a summer's morn I wake,
And open my two eyes,
Out to the clear, born-singing rills
My bird-like spirit flies.

W.H. Davies

I took pleasure in moving, both in the physical effort and in the touch of the air–it was most queer how the air did seem to touch me, even when it was absolutely still. All day long I had a sense of great ease and spaciousness. And my happiness had a strange, remembered quality as though I had lived it before. Oh, how can I recapture it–that utterly right, homecoming sense of recognition? It seems to me now that the whole day was like an avenue leading to a home I had loved once but forgotten, the memory of which was coming back so dimly, so gradually, as I wandered along, that only when my home at last lay before me did I cry: "Now I know why I have been happy!"

Dodie Smith

Happiness

Mental sunshine makes the mind grow, and perpetual happiness makes human nature a flower garden in bloom.

Christian D. Larson

When we feel what we have is enough to make us happy, and that all that surrounds us is as it should be, then we feel peace. Of all the varieties of happiness this is the loveliest.

Welleran Poltarnees

Picture Credits

Front Cover   Alek Plunian. From *Histoire de Pommette*, 1920.

Front Endpapers   Jean Droit. Poster. N.D.

Half Title   Peter Newell. From *Mother Goose's Menagerie*, 1901.

Title Page   Harry B. Neilson. From *Droll Doings*. 1903.

Copyright   Tony Sarg. From *Tony Sarg's Book of Animals*. 1925

Preface   Florence J. & Margaret C. Hoopes. From *The New Day in and Day Out*. 1948.

1   Robert Henri. "Jobie, The Laughing Boy. 1910.

2   Charlotte Steiner. From *Charlotte Steiner's ABC*. 1946.

3   Berta and Elmer Hader. From *Little Elephant*. 1930.

4   Carl Larsson. "Solrosorna" (Sunflowers). 1893.

5   Unknown. Travel poster. N.D.

6   Dennis, Wesley. From *Wagging Tails*. 1955.

7   Louis Moe.

From *Burre-Busses nya äventyr i Trollskogen*. 1918.

8   Frank Schoonover. "Old Man by the Horse." 1915.

9   Leonetto Cappiello. Poster. 1900.

10   John Phillip Falter. Pulp illustration. 1931.

11   Unknown. "A Novel Airship." N.D.

12   Douglass Crockwell.

Advertising illustration. 1951.

13   M. Krestjanoff.

From *Martin et Tommy Installés*. 1920.

14   Campbell Lang.

From *Adventures of Uncle Wiggily:*

The Bunny Rabbit Gentleman with the Twinkling

Pink Nose. 1924.

15   Josh Newton Howitt.

Periodical illustration. N.D.

16   B. Wennerberg. "Kätzchen." 1932.

17   Sarah S. Stilwell Weber. Magazine cover. 1911.

Picture Credits